Frankfurt Airport

Flughafen Frankfurt/Main

Frankfurt Airport

Flughafen Frankfurt/Main

FREDDY BULLOCK

Airlife
England

Copyright © 2001 Freddy Bullock

First published in the UK in 2001
by Airlife Publishing Ltd

**British Library Cataloguing-in-Publication
Data**
  A catalogue record for this book
  is available from the British Library

ISBN 1 84037 269 9

Typeset by Rowland Phototypesetting Ltd, Bury
St Edmunds, Suffolk.
Printed in China.

Airlife Publishing Ltd
101 Longden Road, Shrewsbury, SY3 9EB,
England
E-mail: airlife@airlifebooks.com
Website: www.airlifebooks.com

Flughafen Frankfurt/Main

Frankfurt Airport (FRA) is presently Europe's second largest passenger airport and number one in terms of flown cargo. Located in the heart of Europe, FRA serves as the most important transportation hub on the continent. In global terms, in 1999 Frankfurt ranked number seven in the world for total passengers and number three for international passengers.

During the high season, the aircraft movement activity amounts to more than 1,400 take-offs and landings per day. Some 180,000 passengers travel through Frankfurt Airport on peak days. Thus, nearly 46 million passengers departed from, transferred or landed at continental Europe's busiest commercial airport in 1999. The passenger throughput approached nearly 50 million in 2000. There are more than 100 airlines serving about 260 destinations in 110 countries world-wide – the most extensive global network of any airport.

Frankfurt Airport is owned and operated by Flughafen Frankfurt/Main AG (FAG) – the Frankfurt Airport company (to be renamed Fraport AG in 2001). With a 45.2 per cent stake, the state of Hesse is the company's largest shareholder, followed by the city of Frankfurt with 28.9 per cent and the Federal Republic of Germany with 25.9 per cent. In 2001 the company is planning a partial privatisation via an initial public offering (IPO). FAG is responsible for running what has essentially become a city in itself. More than 460 companies are located at Frankfurt Airport, providing employment to about 62,000 people.

Since the opening of Terminal 1 and the underground railway station in 1972, events have moved on rapidly. In 1994, Terminal 2 and the Sky Line people-mover system connecting both terminals were inaugurated. In March 2000 the Pier A extension of Terminal 1 was opened providing an additional capacity for five million passengers per year.

With the inauguration of FRA's Long-distance Railway Station, the new AIRail Terminal in 1999 Frankfurt Airport has evolved into a full-service 'intermodal travel port' in the middle of Germany where air, rail and road networks are optimally linked. The airport offers excellent rail links: it is directly connected to the regional and long-distance railway plus Germany's high-speed railway system. Many German and European cities such as Berlin, Hanover, Würzburg, Düsseldorf, Cologne, Hamburg, Munich, Vienna, Amsterdam and Basel and many more are served by the German high-speed ICE-trains stopping at the long-distance station. In 2002 FRA will serve as a mainline station on the new ICE line still under construction between Rhine–Main and Rhine–Ruhr economic regions.

Departing from the Regional Railway Station directly accessible from the check-in halls, travellers may reach Frankfurt's city centre within ten minutes as well as major surrounding cities such as Mainz, Wiesbaden or Hanau within approximately half an hour.

The intersection of two of Germany's most important *autobahns*, the A3 and the A5, is adjacent to the airport. The A3 is Germany's main west–east route and the A5 is the most important route linking the north to the south, running all the way down from the most northern tip of Germany to Switzerland.

Frankfurt Airport is Europe's number one cargo gateway and ranks ninth in the world with over 1.5 million tonnes being moved in 1999. The majority of this tonnage, was carried in the holds of passenger aircraft, while freighter aircraft accounted for about 47 per cent.

Germany's overnight hub-and-spoke mail service is based at FRA. Deutsche Post AG, the German Post Office, operates this domestic overnight mail network, moving about 250 tonnes of mail per night to cities throughout Germany. Of course, during the day Frankfurt Airport is also an important airmail gateway – receiving, sorting and distributing airmail from all over the world.

At the southern side of Frankfurt Airport, CargoCity South has been developed during recent years on land that was formerly used by the US Rhine–Main Air Base. Since 1993 this air base area has been gradually returned to the Frankfurt Airport company. The remaining portion that, today, is still being used by the US Air Force will be entirely returned to civilian aviation operations by the end of 2005. The FAG Cargo Terminal was opened in 1997 and subsequently many other handling and cargo-related facilities including an air/rail cargo station. Adjacent to CargoCity South you will find the General Aviation Terminal (GAT) as well as a maintenance building of Lufthansa's Condor subsidiary.

Frankfurt is the home base of Lufthansa German Airlines, FAG's largest partner. With a fleet of over 320 aircraft the airline coordinates all of its global operations from its primary hub at Frankfurt. Every other aircraft landing or taking off from Frankfurt carries the Lufthansa 'Crane' symbol on its tail. Over 300 destinations to 90 countries around the world are served by the airline. In order to allow for smooth and safe business operations substantial maintenance facilities are provided at Frankfurt Airport. Lufthansa Cargo AG is also based at FRA with its fleet of Boeing 747 and McDonnell-Douglas MD-11 freighters.

There are three runways at Frankfurt, Runway North 07L/25R, Runway South 07R/25L (both of which are 4,000 metres in length) and Runway West 18 which is also 4,000 metres in length. It is used for take-offs only, and is usually used by flights with schedules to the east.

The visitors' terraces at Frankfurt Airport's Terminal 1 and 2 are probably the best in the world, and are a popular sight-seeing destination for holidaymakers and aviation enthusiasts alike. Besides viewing aircraft movements, visitors and especially families with children can enjoy extra entertaining facilities and events on the terraces or can take part in an airport tour. It is well worth the visit. As with other books in this airport series the intention is to show the many airlines that visit an airport like Frankfurt, although it is not possible to show every airline for a variety of reasons. However I hope you will enjoy this book.

My thanks go as ever to my wife, Chris, but I am indebted to Robert A. Payne, manager of the International Press Office of FAG for all his help. I am also grateful to my guide Tanya Engelmann and Michael Maurer our driver on the ramp for their valuable assistance. Finally, I would like to thank Captain Hans-Peter Gescher and First Officer Michael Rueckriem for the 'jump seat' trip on their Lufthansa Airbus A319 for my return to Manchester.

Freddy Bullock
Huddersfield, England

Lufthansa Airbus A321-131, D-AIRH proceeds to taxi away from its gate within Terminal 1 towards its take-off runway, 25R.

This aircraft is one of twenty-eight of the type owned by the company.

One of Germany's premier charter companies, Aero-Lloyd, operates a fleet of mainly Airbus aircraft. This A321-231, D-ALAI is painted in a corporate scheme for Trigema, the largest manufacturer of tennis shirts in Europe.

With the airport's ground control tower in the background, Lufthansa's Boeing 747-430, D-ABVH is being loaded prior to its next flight. In common with company practice this aircraft is named after the city of Düsseldorf.

Shosholoza, a Boeing 747-312 registered ZS-SAC of South African Airways, rests during the day, away from the terminals before its return flight to Johannesburg in the evening.

With the distinctive colour scheme of red and white, this LTU Boeing 757-225, D-AMUK sits at the gate within Terminal 2, being loaded before its next charter flight.

Alitalia's McDonnell-Douglas DC-9-82, I-DANP makes it way to the westerly Runway 18 for its take-off position operating Flight AZ 405, the 15.20 departure to Rome–Fiumicino.

Royal Air Maroc Boeing 737-4B6, CN-RNC taxies to the gate at Terminal 1 with Flight AT 816 from the Moroccan city of Nador.

Glinting in the morning sun is the tail of
American Airlines' Boeing 777 N791AN.

Middle East Airlines' (MEA) Airbus A310-222, 3B-STI, taxies from the gate within Terminal 1 on Flight 218 to Beirut. Lebanon's national symbol, the cedar tree adorns the tail.

Flight PS 401 from Kiev has landed on time and makes its way to a satellite stand in Terminal 2. Ukraine International Boeing 737-247, UR-GAC looks very attractive in its white, blue and yellow scheme.

With the tow tractor attached, Kuwait Airways' Airbus A340-313, 9K-ANA is in push-back mode. Flight KU 172 will return to Kuwait City in a journey lasting around 6 hours 40 minutes.

RIGHT:
With a fleet of over thirty aircraft, this Airbus A310-222, F-OGYW is the only western-built aircraft flown by Armenian Airlines. Flight RME 104 will depart for the country's capital, Yerevan, at 15.25. Note the Mercedes being loaded.

BELOW:
Named *Torsten Viking*, Scandinavian Airlines' DC-9-87, SE-DIU taxies for take-off.

Meridiana's McDonnell-Douglas MD-82
EI-CRW taxies past the spectators' terrace
at Terminal 1 on its way to Runway 18 on
Flight IG 956 to Olbia in northern Sardinia.

In push-back mode from Gate B28, Lufthansa Boeing 747-430, D-ABVC, named after the city of Baden-Württemburg, looks in good shape for its forthcoming flight to the Far East.

Condor Flugdienst is a subsidiary of Lufthansa operating both scheduled and charter flights to many parts of the world. This Condor Berlin Airbus A320-212, D-AICG shows the newly revised colour scheme adopted by the company

A long-time operator of the Boeing 737, Lufthansa today has over seventy-eight examples in its fleet. D-ABEL *Pforzheim* is a series 300.

LEFT:
One of Hapag-Lloyd's new Boeing 737-8K5s, D-AHFD sits at the gate within the new Terminal 1 extension opened in July 2000.

BELOW:
N416FE, an Airbus A310-222F of the world's largest parcel carrier, FedEx, waits all day on the ramp before its evening flight to Subic Bay in the Philippines with a stop *en route*. Prior to its conversion this aircraft was registered as N801PA of Pan Am.

Looking resplendent in the morning sun, CSA Czech Airlines Boeing 737-45S, OK-EGP awaits instructions to proceed on Flight OK 535 to the Czech capital, Prague. Having given the thumbs-up to the captain that everything is clear, the ground handler walks away.

Flying three times weekly between the
Colombian capital, Bogota, and Frankfurt,
Avianca's Boeing 767-259ER, N986AN sits
at Gate C8 between flights.

RIGHT:
Eurowings' Airbus A319-112, D-AKNI is having some light maintenance carried out before the start of its next charter flight. This company, based in Nuremberg, operates scheduled and charter services.

BELOW:
US Airways was the first United States airline to use the Airbus A330-300 series aircraft. Only a few months old, N672UW is seen at Terminal 2 operating Flight US 781 to Pittsburgh.

Russian-built Yakovlev Yak-42D, ER-YCB of
Air Moldova International is seen here
operating Flight RM 864 to Chisinau, the
country's capital city.

RIGHT:
There are two fire stations at Frankfurt Airport, one adjacent to Terminal 1 and the other on the south-west perimeter of the field. Shown here are examples of the rescue equipment in use.

BELOW:
This new Swedish airline, Jet 2000, was using its sole aircraft, an Embraer ERJ-145 registered SE-RAA, on services to and from East Midlands on behalf of British Midland in August 2000.

Three distinctive tail schemes adorn these Boeing 757 and 767 models belonging to LTU, Delta and British Airways, the latter wearing the 'Chelsea Rose' tail scheme.

After its push-back from Gate D5, this Boeing 767-332ER N1603 belonging to Delta Air Lines taxies towards its take-off position from Runway 25R on Flight DL 015 to Atlanta, Georgia.

With the Sky Line people-mover clearly visible in the background, Lufthansa's Boeing 747-230B, D-ABYX moves slowly into its final position at Gate B20 at Terminal 1 before its engines are shut down and the ground crews take over.

Requiring extra capacity during summer 2000, Swissair was using its Airbus A330-223 on the morning flights between Frankfurt and Zurich. HB-IQC taxies away from Terminal 2 for a 10.10 departure.

Flight TK 1588 from Frankfurt to Istanbul is a daily service operated by Turkish Airlines, usually by an Airbus A310-304, as on this occasion, when TC-JDC was the aircraft. It is seen at the gate within Terminal 1.

With the demise of its Boeing 737s, Croatia Airlines now boasts a fleet of Airbus A319s and A320s. The airline's latest acquisition, 9A-CTL, is an A319-112, seen about to start Flight OU 411 to Zagreb.

RIGHT:
Varig's Flight RG 740 from Rio de Janeiro and São Paulo arrives in mid-afternoon. When all unloading has taken place the aircraft is towed to a satellite stand for a few hours before its evening departure. McDonnell-Douglas MD-11 PP-VQH is the aircraft flying today's service.

Boeing 737-5C9, LX-LGP of Luxair has arrived with Flight LG 9305 from the city and Duchy of Luxembourg and taxies quickly to its gate in Terminal 1.

Increasingly popular with airlines for use on their low-volume routes is the new range of smaller commuter jets. Maersk Air of Copenhagen use their Canadair CRJ-200ER on weekday services between Billund in Denmark and Frankfurt. Flight DM 266 waits on the ramp for its departure at 14.10.

ABOVE:
This Boeing 737-7B6, CN-RNR of Royal Air Maroc, is a mere five months old. With a lightweight tractor attached, the aircraft is pushed back from Gate B23 in Terminal 1. Flight AT 811 to Casablanca is a daily service.

LEFT:
Hapag-Lloyd, one of Germany's premier charter companies, is rapidly introducing its new Boeing 737-8K5s, giving the airline increased capacity. D-AHFO is such an example and is seen arriving at Terminal 1 with a charter flight from Majorca.

Icelandair's latest Boeing 757-208, TF-FIP, looks superb in the company's new colour scheme introduced in 1999. With Terminal 2 in the background and push-back complete, Flight FI 521 waits for instructions to taxi at the start of its flight to Reykjavik.

OPPOSITE:
The tails featured here belong to Boeing 737s of Ukraine International and Malév and a Condor Boeing 767.

With engines running, this vintage Balkan Cargo Antonov An-12B, LZ-BAF is ready for departure. It is named *River of Maritza* after a major waterway in Bulgaria.

LEFT:
The midday departure, Flight SQ 025 to Singapore by the country's airline will, on this occasion, be flown by Boeing 747-412, 9V-SML. After its push-back from Gate B23 it will taxi to the westerly Runway 18 for take-off.

BELOW:
With passengers and luggage aboard, this Tunisair Airbus A320-211 TS-IML is ready for departure to the city of Tunis on Flight TU 745.

Airbus A321-111, F-GTAE, of the French
national airline Air France, sits by the gate
at Terminal 2 whilst it is serviced in
preparation for the morning's 10.40
departure to Paris – Charles de Gaulle.

LEFT:
Lufthansa CityLine is the commuter arm of the parent company, with a fleet of smaller jet aircraft. Avro RJ185 D-AVRD sits in the afternoon sun awaiting its next flight.

BELOW:
A former Russian state, Belarus is now a separate republic. The country's airline Belavia operates a fleet of former Aeroflot aircraft. Flight BRU 894 to Minsk is flown by Tupolev Tu-134A, EW 65108.

The final baggage is put on board this Boeing 737-45S, OK-EGP of the Czech airline CSA before its flight to Prague.

LEFT:
On the south side of the airfield, part of the old USAF base already handed over to the airport authority is the General Aviation Terminal (GAT), which caters for all private flights. Avanti Air's Beech 1900C, D-CARA is operating such a flight.

BELOW:
In mid-morning, three American Airlines aircraft and one belonging to Lufthansa are lined-up in Terminal 1's Section C.

RIGHT:
A Boeing 767-33AER, D-AMUP of Düsseldorf-based LTU arrives at Terminal 2 at the end of its flight.

BELOW:
At the end of its international flight Lufthansa's Boeing 747-230B (SCD), D-ABYX taxies slowly to Gate B20 in Terminal 1.

With only six Airbus A310-304s left in service with the airline, Lufthansa's D-AIDL is pushed back from the gate at Terminal 1.

United Airlines' Boeing 777-222ER has recently landed after its overnight flight from the United States and awaits instructions to proceed to its gate at Terminal 1.

OPPOSITE:
This view, taken from the superb observation deck on Pier A at Terminal 1, shows two Lufthansa Boeing 747s and the ground control air traffic centre.

ABOVE:
7T-VHL is one of two Lockheed L100-30 Hercules transport aircraft used by Air Algérie and is seen at the western end of the airfield between flights.

BELOW:
On a beautiful August morning Cyprus Airways' Airbus A320-231, 5B-DAT is next to land on Runway 25L with Flight CY 376 from Larnaca.

Formerly with Air France as a passenger-carrier, this Airbus A300B4-203F was converted to cargo configuration and is now in use with HeavyLift Cargo Airlines of Stansted, England. G-HLAB taxies out of the Lufthansa cargo complex to commence its flight.

With an El Al Boeing 757 in the foreground, an Avro RJ70, YL-BAL, of Air Baltic taxies towards its stand after a flight from Latvian capital, Riga.

Airbus A340-311 4R-ADB displays Sri Lankan's latest colour scheme whilst operating the UL 558 service to Colombo.

Wearing additional decals declaring 'Dubai Summer Surprise 2000', Emirates' Airbus A330-243, A6-EKW arrives with the daily flight from Dubai.

ABOVE:
This Yakovlev Yak-42, RA-42375 of Avialinii Kubani (Kuban Airlines) is ready to depart to its home base of Krasnodar in Russia.

RIGHT:
Airbus A321-211, EC-HAC is seen on finals after flying from Madrid on Flight IB 3500, a daily service to Frankfurt.

Tyrolean Airways' Fokker F70, OE-LFJ waits on the ramp before setting off on Flight VO 464 to Salzburg.

RIGHT:
Canadian charter company Air Transat's
aircraft are regular visitors to Frankfurt. The
company's Boeing 757-23A, C-GTSE is
seen at Gate B47 during loading.

OPPOSITE:
Lufthansa's Boeing 747-430 crosses the A5
autobahn on its final approach to Runway
25L.

BELOW:
In superb evening light Korean Air Boeing
747-4B5, HL 7409 taxies to Gate E4 at
Terminal 2 at the end of its non-stop flight
from the South Korean capital, Seoul.

RIGHT:
A front-end view of Avianca's Boeing 767-259ER, N986AN.

BELOW:
The daily morning service from Athens, OA 165, is about to land on Runway 25L flown by Olympic Airways' Boeing 737-484, SX-BKD.

With all ground vehicles removed and a tow tractor attached, this KLM cityhopper, Fokker F70 PH-KZA, is ready for push-back from the gate at Terminal 2.

To promote the Hannover Expo 2000 Trade Show, Lufthansa painted advertising decals onto its Boeing 747-430, D-ABVK, which appropriately is named *Hannover*.

ABOVE:
With over thirty Airbus A340s in the Lufthansa fleet, predominantly series 300 models, there are six A340-211s, one of which, D-AIGD, is seen here taxiing to its gate in Terminal 1.

LEFT:
El Al's Boeing 757-258, 4X-EBR looks in good shape to land on Runway 25L to complete Flight LY 357 from Tel Aviv.

ABOVE:
In conjunction with Lufthansa, Air Dolomiti operates its ATR 72-212As on services to and from the Italian city of Verona. I-ADLT taxies for take-off on Flight EN 2710.

BELOW:
Pakistan International (PIA) Airbus A310-308, AP-BEQ sits at Gate C5 in Terminal 1 before its flight to Karachi.

Air Canada's Airbus A340-313X, C-FYLC, on Flight AC 876 from Toronto, looks in perfect trim as it prepares to land on runway 25L.

Canadair RJ100ER, F-GRJC of French regional carrier Brit Air is one of several operated on behalf of Air France which regularly visit Frankfurt.

Complete with a '2000' motif, this Trans-aero Airlines Boeing 737-7K9, N100UN has recently arrived from Moscow on the daily service UN 709.

Estonian Air's Boeing 737-5Q8, ES-ABC taxies past the spectators' terrace on a dull afternoon operating Flight OV 162 to Tallinn.

ABOVE:
Wearing additional titles to celebrate the King's 72nd Birthday Celebrations, Thai Airways' Boeing 747-4D7, HS-TGT is towed to Gate B20, before the start of Flight TG 921 to Bangkok.

RIGHT:
With the 'Union Flag' tail scheme, British Airways' Airbus A319-131, G-EUPF taxies away from Terminal 2 with the midday flight to Birmingham.

Japan Airlines' Flight JL 407 from Tokyo–Narita has landed and approaches its gate at Terminal 2 in the late afternoon. JA 8078, a Boeing 747-446, is the aircraft on today's service.

With a stop in Abu Dhabi, the twice-weekly service from Taiwan is under the flight code AE 061, the designation of Mandarin Airlines. However its three MD-11s have been absorbed into China Airlines' fleet. B-18152 has already been repainted in China Airlines' colours, and is seen on arrival at Terminal 2.

OPPOSITE:
Lufthansa's famous 'Crane' symbol is seen on the tail-section of Airbus A300B4-605R, D-AIAW.

Northwest's daily morning service to
Detroit departs at 10.20 as Flight NW 053.
McDonnell-Douglas DC-10-40, N159US
has been given the all-clear by ground
control and awaits instructions from the
tower.

LEFT:
With only eight Boeing 'Classic' 747-230Bs left in service, Lufthansa will soon cease operating the type. Meanwhile, D-ABYQ is still in excellent shape after twenty-two years in service.

BELOW:
Royal Jordanian Airlines' Airbus A320-211, bearing the French registration, F-OGYA and named *Cairo*, has night-stopped in Frankfurt and will soon be towed back to the terminal to operate Flight RJ 122 to Amman.

Arriving with the daily flight from Moscow–Sheremetyevo, Aeroflot Russian International Airlines' Airbus A310-324, F-OGYV, is seen turning in to Gate C8 at Terminal 1.

BELOW:
Italian charter and scheduled airline Air One was operating this French-registered Boeing 737-3M8, F-GKTA, on a non-scheduled service when this picture was taken.

With all available doors open to let in 'fresh air', this Garuda Indonesia Airlines Boeing 747-4U3, PK-GSH sits adjacent to Lufthansa's cargo terminal for the day, before its evening flight back to Jakarta.

Wearing the new livery of El Al, this Boeing
757-258ER, 4X-EBU, is seen passing the
observation area on Flight LY 358 to Tel
Aviv.

LEFT:
Based at Innsbruck, Austrian airline Tyrolean Airways' aircraft are frequent visitors to Frankfurt. The next flight to Salzburg will be flown by this DHC-8-106, OE-LLE, fitted with around thirty-eight seats.

BELOW:
Wearing the 'Union Flag' scheme on its tail, British Airways' Boeing 767-336ER, G-BNWY is making the long taxi to Runway 7L for take-off on a flight to London–Heathrow.

ZK-NZX is one of only two Boeing 747-219Bs left in Air New Zealand's fleet, the majority having been replaced by the later series 400. In June 1998 the aircraft is seen in push-back mode from Terminal 2 at the start of Flight NZ 019 over the northern polar route to Los Angeles, its only stop before its long journey over the Pacific Ocean to Auckland.

Pamplona-based Spanish air taxi company Aerovento operates two Swearingen SA226TC Metros on charters all over Europe. EC-HCU is seen parked on the south side of the airfield awaiting its return to Spain.

A division of KLM uk, Buzz, with its attractive yellow colours is a relatively new airline offering cheap tickets to consumers. BAe 146-300, G-UKRC is operating the mid-afternoon flight back to its base at London–Stansted.

With the tractor attached Malaysia Airlines' Boeing 747-4H6, 9M-MPH is slowly pushed back from the gate at Terminal 2 to start its flight to Kuala Lumpur under code MH 005.

Lufthansa Cargo's Boeing 747-230B, D-ABYZ, fitted with a side cargo-door, is receiving some attention at the company's maintenance section.

Polar Air Cargo's Boeing 747s are seen in many airports around the world. N922FT is a series 200 which arrived from New York in the early morning. It will return later in the evening.

KLM cityhopper's Fokker F70, PH-KZA, arrives from Amsterdam Schiphol on a Saturday afternoon when loads are lighter. This justifies the use of the smaller aircraft on a service normally operated by Boeing 737-400s.

OPPOSITE:
Qantas and Cathay Pacific tails.

ABOVE:
With Terminal 2 in the background, US Airways' Boeing 767-2B7ER, N656US moves away with the daily flight to Philadelphia under the flight code US 893.

RIGHT:
A front-end study of Cathay Pacific's Boeing 747-467, B-HOZ.

Painted in the colours of the Polish Airline LOT, this ATR 72-202, SP-LFD is leased to and operated by Eurolot on regional services. In evening sunshine the 17.40 flight to Breslau, LO 366, is moved away from its stand at Terminal 2.

Balkan Bulgarian Airlines was using this rather shabby-looking Tupolev Tu-154M, LZ-LTX on its service to Sofia when this picture was taken in August 2000.

LEFT:
Owned and operated in Team Lufthansa colours by Augsburg Airways, this Dash DHC-8-103A, D-BIER waits between flights at the small commuter area just east of Terminal 2.

BELOW:
Frankfurt's long-distance railway station opened in 1999. It is operated by Deutsch Bundesbahn and has proved a great success. An Inter City Express is seen here on a service to Altona station in Hamburg.

Japan Airlines' flight from Osaka, JA 427, has recently arrived in Frankfurt and is seen turning onto the centre line to park at Gate D8 in Terminal 2. JAL's 'J-Bird', McDonnell-Douglas MD-11, JA 8582 is named *Tancho (Red Crowned Crane)*, after a native Japanese bird.

With the all-glass frontage of Terminal 2 behind it, British Airways' Boeing 767-336ER, G-BNWT, wearing the Scottish-inspired tail scheme featuring 'Benyhone' tartan awaits its taxi instructions to commence Flight BA 905 to London –Heathrow.

Spanair is one of Spain's premier charter companies. McDonnell-Douglas DC-9-82, EC-HJB, is seen leaving Terminal 1 to start its flight to Palma de Mallorca.

In common with the early-morning arrivals of some other airlines, Air Namibia's flight from Windhoek is towed from the terminal area after unloading, and spends the day at a satellite parking-area prior to its evening departure. Boeing 747-48E, V5-NMA is the company's latest acquisition, replacing its Boeing 747SP.

LEFT:
With stops in São Paulo, Brazil and Madrid, LAN Chile's flight from the country's capital Santiago, LA 700, arrives in Frankfurt on time at 17.40. Wearing the airline's relatively new colours, Boeing 767-319ER, CC-CZT taxies to its arrival gate in Terminal 2.

BELOW:
This view of US Airways' Airbus A330-323X, N670UW was shot against the backdrop of the glass-fronted Terminal 2. The splendid observation deck is seen above the aircraft.

Pulkovo Aviation, based in St Petersburg, flies a thrice-weekly service to Frankfurt. On this occasion Tupolev Tu-154M, RA-85767 was the aircraft operating Flight PLK 656.

In Scandinavian Airlines System's new colours, Boeing 737-683, LN-RPZ waits whilst its intended gate position is cleared.

With twelve of the new Boeing 757-330s now in service, Condor Flugdienst was the first airline to use this new type. In the airline's new colours, D-ABOI rests awhile between flights.

Probably the most attractively painted Lockheed VC-130H Hercules you will see anywhere is this Saudi Arabian example HZ-114. Parked on the south side of the airfield, this aircraft is used by the country's special flight services.

السعودية

SAUDI ARABIAN

HZ-114

Named after the Bavarian town of Landshut, this Lufthansa Airbus A319-114, D-AILK passes the company's cargo complex *en route* for take-off.

Air Zimbabwe's Boeing 767-2N0ER, Z-WPF
has been towed from the western end of
the airport and approaches its gate at
Terminal 2. Later in the evening it will
depart on Flight UM 727 to Harare.

LEFT:
A front-end view of Lufthansa's Boeing 747-230B, D-ABYX.

BELOW:
British Midland Flight BD 664 to Birmingham is almost loaded and ready for departure at 14.10. Boeing 737-37Q, G-ODSK looks stylish in the afternoon sun.

ABOVE:
Continental Airlines' daily service to New York – Newark is now flown by its Boeing 777-224ER. N78001 is operating Flight CO 051.

BELOW:
This Boeing 737-2T4, LY-BSD, of Lithuanian Airlines, taxies to Runway 18 for departure with Flight TE 421 to Vilnius.

ABOVE:
Air Moldova International is one of the national airlines of several former Russian states that use ex-Aeroflot aircraft. Yakovlev Yak-42D, ER-YCA, now in the new colours of the airline waits before its return to Chisinau.

LEFT:
Delivered new in March 2000, this Airbus A321-231, D-ALAM of Aero Lloyd has just arrived on Flight YP 4119 from Thessaloniki in Greece.

With four daily services from and to
Vienna, Austrian Airlines' Airbus A321-211,
OE-LBE is seen with the second flight of
the day, OS 124.

LEFT:
On a bright August morning, Lufthansa's Airbus A340-313X, D-AIGO prepares to land on Runway 25L at the end of its flight.

BELOW:
A vintage Viscount V.814, rarely seen outside the confines of Lufthansa's maintenance area. With two props missing, as the title suggests, it is used for training.

Turkish charter company, Sun Express, in which Lufthansa has an interest, operates to holiday resorts in Turkey. Boeing 737-3YO, TC-SUR is about to depart on such a flight.

Presently leased from BWIA International, this Airbus A321-131, TC-ALO of Turkish charter airline Air Alfa waits on the ramp at Frankfurt on a dull day.

This night shot illustrates the action on the floodlit ramp during the loading and unloading of mail on behalf of Deutsche Post. By two o'clock in the morning 250 metric tons of mail will have been handled and all the aircraft involved will have left, leaving the airport quiet until dawn. *(FAG)*

Since receiving attention to its inner starboard engine, new covers have been fitted in plain grey. Apart from that, the Aboriginal-inspired artwork entitled 'Wanula Dreaming' still draws the eye towards Qantas' Boeing 747-438, VH-OJB. It will fly to Sydney via Singapore in the evening.

The air traffic controller has unlimited views of the airfield and its surrounds. From the control tower situated in the south-west corner of the airfield, the controllers are in contact with landing aircraft before they are visible, and handle all traffic until it is on the ground. After landing, the aircraft is handed over to ground control, based in the tower above Terminal 1. *(FAG)*

One of the many Lufthansa check-in gates in Terminal 1. *(FAG)*

A Thai Airways jumbo climbs into the sky on departure from Frankfurt. The ground-lights seen are for aircraft landing in the opposite direction. *(FAG)*

LEFT:
Air Canada's second service of the day to Toronto, Flight AC 873, will be flown by its Boeing 747-433 (SCD) C-GAGL, which is seen during the push-back procedure.

BELOW:
American Airlines' 'Triple Seven' is surrounded by ground-handling equipment during preparations for its flight across the Atlantic to Dallas–Fort Worth.

In this birds-eye view of Pier A at Terminal 1, the superb observation deck is clearly seen. *(FAG)*